Healing Inn Silence: You Have The Strength Inside You, Don't You Know?

Disclaimer: This books content is not claiming to solve any problem or be a replacement for professional help. This content is not claiming that any person will recover from depression or any other mental health disorders, nor is it claiming that a person will gain mental or emotional stability by reading this book. The content by no means suggesting a person to feel, act or do anything else in a way that can affect a person's life. It is a written personal experience and conversational piece only.

Written By-Healur

Dedicated to all my supporters and those who struggle with mental health.

Table Of Contents

Introduction

Have you ever felt alone and lost in your struggles with depression? Have you ever experienced negative thoughts that consume your mind and make it difficult to see the light at the end of the tunnel? Have you ever struggled with unstable relationships and wondered if you will ever find love and stability?

If you answered yes to any of these questions, then I understand how you feel. I have been there too. I know the struggles, the pain, and the loneliness that comes with these challenges.

But I also know that it is possible to heal, to grow, and to find happiness and peace of mind. I have learned how to cope and manage my emotions and relationships better, and I want to share my thoughts and experiences with you.

In this book, I will share my journey, my struggles, and the lessons I have learned along the way. I hope that my words will bring you comfort and encouragement, and that you will know that you are not alone in your journey.

No matter where you are in your life right now, know that it is possible to heal, grow, and find happiness.

With Love & Hope,

Healur

CHAPTER ONE

I never realized how much you being in & out of my life affected me,

Left me with constant doubt.

Until I found myself clinging to any form of affection

. Desperate for love, seeking any connection.

When I truly needed, what I truly craved the most

Was the kind of love that only a father can give you when you need

it the most.

I needed your presence, your guidance, and care.

To have you by my side, to know that you're there.

Expressing Things, I Feared Saying, Part One

Having a father's guidance in life,

Is something that I didn't realize you needed,

Until I needed guidance and had to wipe away my own tears from my eyes.

If only I had you to guide me to show me how to be treated right,

I could have been saved from so many heartaches,

Despite the pain that came my way, I found my strength.

I cried alone, but I got through it all,

Without you there to catch me when I fall.

Now though I wish things were different,

My journey has taught me to

find guidance and strength from within

and has given me many valuable life lessons.

Expressing Things, I Feared Saying, Part Two

Once I cared with all my heart,
But it always tore me apart,
For every time I gave my all,
I found myself in an endless fall.

My kindness was taken for granted,
My love was disregarded,
And so, to protect myself
I allowed my heart to become restrained.

Deep down, I'm still that sweet soul,
Starving for attention that makes me whole,
I long for a love I should have received,
The little affection that I so desperately needed.

Expressing Things, I Feared Saying, Part Three

Invisible wounds, hidden from view,
The saddest part is no one knew.
They say time heals, but doubts starts to creep,
Will the pain fade, or will it forever run deep?

Carrying burdens too heavy to hold,
Though smiles may mask the tears I cry,
Inside, the pain refuses to die.

Expressing Things, I Feared Saying, Part Four

In a bubble, you feel so alone,
Isolated & trapped, in your own thoughts,
It's hard to breathe, hard to see,
When it feels like no one hears you.

You try to break free from the confines of your mind,
but the weight of your emotions holds you down.
The world around you become a blur
as you struggle to make sense of it all.
Friends and family pass by, oblivious
to the invisible barriers that surround you.

You reach out for help, but your voice gets lost
in the vastness of the universe.
You long for someone to understand,
to hear your silent cries for connection.
But all you get in return is a hollow echo,
bouncing back from the walls of your isolation.

Days turn into weeks, and weeks into months.
Time seems to stand still while you remain
trapped in your own thoughts.
The laughter of others becomes a painful reminder

of the happiness you long for.

You watch as life goes on,

feeling like a spectator in your own existence.

Expressing Things, I Feared Saying, Part Five

I stayed up the entire night,
Laying in bed with my phone.
Hoping and praying for a sign,
That I'm not all alone.

The silence was deafening,
And the emptiness unbearable.
I wanted someone to hear me,
And let me into their heart.

My heart ached with pain,
I needed someone's attention.
I was desperate for validation,
From someone's affection.

But somewhere deep inside,
I knew that I couldn't survive.
Depending on others for my joy,
And feeling so deprived

The memories haunted me,
Of putting their needs before my own.
It only left me feeling empty,

And feeling painfully alone.

It was time to face the truth,
And break the chains holding me down.
I had to start loving myself,
And finally turn my life around.

And so I promised myself,
To no longer seek their praise.
Instead, I'll focus on me,
And find my own unique ways.

CHAPTER TWO

Love can be a fairytale, but sometimes it's just an illusion.
I dreamt big and fell hard, but you were never my conclusion.

Escaping The Darkness, Part One

I felt so in love right from the start & I knew that you would have my heart. Love at first sight, it's now so clear; that you're the one I held so dear.

Escaping The Darkness, Part Two

Each day that goes on, a constant reminder
Of the spark of the love, we once shared.
Of hope that maybe someday you'll return to me
And take the loneliness and heartache away.

Without you by my side, the world seems colder,
The colors seem dull, and the days seem older than they should be,
For time moves slow but does not hesitate to move on
When you're not here, my heart seems to know.

The laughter that once filled the air between us
Now replaced by silence, a hollow emptiness that's so vast
I wonder if we'll ever find a way to bridge the distance that grew between us.

Escaping The Darkness, Part Three

Love blinded me;
I couldn't see the pain you caused so endlessly.
Tears fell as you took it out on me, without a doubt.
I loved you so much, I couldn't leave
no matter how many times you continued to do this to me.

Even though you hurt me continuously.
You hurt me in every way,
I couldn't walk away; I was trapped,
But now I see, I'm finally free from the pain you caused so endlessly.

Escaping The Darkness, Part Four

Grieving for someone still alive,
A pain that's hard to comprehend,
A love that I cannot contrive,
A heart that will not easily mend.

I want to give all my love to you,
But deep down I know it's in vain.
You wouldn't do the same, it's true
Only causing me more pain.

I wish you could feel and see,
The agony you put me through,
But you continue to live your life carefree,
Without a thought of what you did to me.

I wish I could just stop caring, & unlove you with ease,
But all my efforts are quite daring,
As my heart still longs for you to please.

Escaping The Darkness, Part Five

I thought I had no other choice,
But to stay with you and ignore the noise.
The noise of my own intuition,
Telling me to leave this toxic situation.

It took time, but eventually, I learned,
That my love for you had to be returned.
Love was not meant to inflict pain,
It shouldn't leave us scarred and drained.

I finally found the strength to walk away,
To leave the toxicity behind & embrace a brighter day.
I took control and put myself first,
I put my healing and happiness above the worst.

It was very difficult, but I'm glad I did,
I learned that my happiness should never be hidden.
That true love doesn't hurt and cause pain,
It shouldn't leave scars or make you feel insane.

Escaping The Darkness, Part Six

It's hard to admit, even to yourself,
When love becomes abuse, and your heart is no longer well.
A relationship that once felt so right,
Suddenly became a never-ending fight.

You insisted you loved me
and gave me the world,
But neglect, control, and manipulation
were the only things you provided in this love.
I was trapped in a relationship that made me feel small,
And I couldn't talk to anyone,
not even those who cared for me above all.

Escaping The Darkness, Part Seven

After all this, I decided to give up the fantasy, I once had about you in my mind. I have given up on the perfect picture, I once painted for you. I accept you for who you are, and I will never look back again.

CHAPTER THREE

A new beginning...

True love isn't about finding someone who completes you. Instead, someone who accepts and embraces every imperfect part of you.

Searching For You, Part One

I often wonder where you are,
If you're close or if you're far.
But every night, before I sleep,
I pray your love I'll keep.

I sense your existence, a palpable energy,
In my heart, I'm certain we're destined to be.
Even though I haven't met you yet,
My love for you is strong, I won't forget.

I search for you in every face,
In the crowds and in different places.
But time has not revealed you to me,
I hold on to faith, that one day we'll meet.

Until then, I'll keep searching,
And each day my heart will keep longing
For the day when our love will start,
And we'll never be apart.

Searching For You, Part Two

Every day I'm looking for clues
A sign that you're near and true.
I long for the day that we meet,
And our hearts merge into one beat.

Wherever you may be,
Know that I am always here.
Waiting for my soulmate,
To come and wipe away my tears.

Searching For You, Part Three

Your smile became the light on my darkest days,
Your laughter fills me with joy always.
I never knew how complete I could be,
Until you came and completed me.

I can't imagine my life without you,
You bring me happiness and make my heart renew.
You are my soulmate, my partner in crime,
Together we will conquer time.

I promise to love you forever and always,
To support and cherish you in all ways.
You are my light in the darkest hour,
In your arms is where I find my power.

Thank you for being my heart's desire,
For igniting a flame that will never retire.
I love you more than words can express,
You fill my life with love and happiness.

Searching For You, Part Four

I promise to always love you true,

To always be there for you,

In all life's moments, big and small,

I'll be there to catch you when you fall.

Searching For You, Part Five

Your love taught me that imperfections are not barriers to being loved, but rather opportunities for genuine connection.

Searching For You, Part Six

I thank the stars above every single day,

For bringing me to you in every way.

My heart is filled with love and gratitude,

I am blessed to have you as my soulmate, dude.

It wasn't until we crossed paths

That I experienced what love truly is.

Searching For You, Part Seven

Loving you is a choice that has no regrets. It has taught me that sometimes it's not always about how much you love someone; it's about how that person makes you feel. Within your love, my soul is always brought back to life.

Searching For You, Part Eight

I'm not sure if destiny exists, but the moment we met, it was almost as if this was exactly where we both needed to be. We were exactly what we both needed, as if we were designed perfectly for each other: We met each other in the divine time.

CHAPTER FOUR

I know it's hard when you love someone so deeply and invest so much effort in them, because of your genuine love. Remember this: you are important and deserve to be given the respect, and love that you offer to others. Don't allow love to consume you to the point where you forget that you are worthy of being loved, just as much as you give love to others.

If someone truly loves you, they will value and respect you, treating you in the way that you deserve. Never settle or accept anything less than what you deserve. Every time you allow someone to disrespect you or intentionally hurt you, you are sending them a message that you accept their lack of love for you. By doing this, you are telling them that it's okay to treat you that way. Only when you learn to respect and value yourself will you find a love that is true and everlasting.

A Better Way, Part One

It's important to trust yourself and your instincts, even when no one else does. You have to know that you're capable of achieving anything you set your mind to, and once you believe in your abilities, the universe conspires to help you achieve your dreams.

So, my message to you is to believe in yourself, trust your instincts, and work hard towards your dreams. Never give up on yourself, no matter how difficult the road ahead may seem. Your belief in yourself is the first step towards achieving your dreams, and everything else will fall into place once you believe in yourself.

A Better Way, Part Two

I know that sometimes it gets so hard that you don't know if you'll have the strength to continue or move forward to the next day. But remember the time you felt this way before it was difficult to get through, but you made it to today. So, if you did it once, you'll be able to do it again. You got this! Whatever you're going through, you'll get over it. So, when you feel another tough day, remember that you've made it through a tough day before, which means you are capable of making it through another one. You got this! In time, you'll feel better once again.

A Better Way, Part Three

Life is a journey filled with uncertainty, comprised of highs and lows, sudden twists, and unforeseeable changes in direction. At times, we may feel like we are on top of the world, and everything is going according to plan. Other times, we may feel like we are being pulled down by the weight of our problems and struggles.

It is during these challenging moments in life that we are forced to grow and learn. Whether we like it or not, adversity is a part of life, and it is how we choose to approach it that will determine both our present and our future.

The most challenging experiences in life are also the ones that contain the most crucial lessons to listen to. These are the moments when we are pushed out of our comfort zone, forced to confront our fears, and challenged to overcome our limitations. They are what teach us resilience, strength, and perseverance. They are what mold us into the person we are meant to be.

When we are faced with difficult times, it is easy to feel defeated and discouraged. We may feel like giving up or just accepting that things will never get better. However, it is important not to lose sight of the bigger picture. Every challenge we face, no matter how big or small, has the potential to teach us something important about ourselves, others, and the world around us.

A Better Way, Part Four

It is always okay to say 'no', to set boundaries; it's important. Never lose yourself in the act of giving: Remember; you're responsible for yourself alone. While setting boundaries may invite questions, those who truly love you will respect them.

A Better Way, Part Five

You made it this far. You have survived the darkest moments in your life, and you are still standing. You are a survivor, a fighter, and an overcomer. You are capable of achieving greatness, no matter what obstacles come your way.

It's okay to feel uncertain about what the future holds. Throughout our lives, we inevitably encounter moments of doubt and uncertainty. However, it is vital to consistently reinforce within yourself the understanding that you possess incredible strength, remarkable capabilities, and the power to triumph over any hurdle. Refuse to let fear become a barrier that hinders you from reaching your dreams and aspirations.

Embrace the uncertainty, focus on your goals, and take each day as it comes. Believe in yourself, and do not let anyone or anything discourage you. Keep pushing forward. The road ahead may be tough, but with time, perseverance, and a positive mindset, you will emerge victorious.

Made in the USA
Columbia, SC
18 September 2023